AF251972

BIBLE PROMISES
for Soul-winners
James Ryan

Leila — praying for
you regularly.
Trust all is well.
Love —
Myrna ☺

BROADMAN PRESS
Nashville, Tennessee

© Copyright 1988 • Broadman Press
All rights reserved
4250-71
ISBN: 0-8054-5071-8

Dewey Decimal Classification: 248.5
Subject Heading: WITNESSING
Library of Congress Catalog Card Number: 88-22975

Printed in the United States of America

Library of Congress Cataloging-in-Publication Data

Ryan, James, 1940-
  Bible promises for soul-winners / James Ryan.
    p.   cm.
  ISBN 0-8054-5071-8 (pbk.)
  1. Evangelistic work—Biblical teaching. 2. Witness
bearing (Christianity)—Biblical teaching.   I. Title.
BS680.E86R93   1989
248′.5—dc19   88-22975

Contents

Introduction

You have picked up this book because you are interested in soul-winning. There are many passages that focus on God's plan to use you in winning a lost world. This promise book is filled with Scripture references which speak to that endeavor. What will you do about opportunities that come your way to win others to Christ? Only you can answer. My prayer is that this book will encourage, challenge, and assist you in soul-winning.

Soul-winning has become the life-style of many contemporary Christians. It was the pattern of Jesus and His followers. Everywhere they went, they searched for persons to share the good news. Everyone they met was a potential follower of Jesus. There were no exceptions. No wonder the early church grew at such an amazing and miraculous rate. God honored their efforts.

New Testament writers multiplied their efforts at soul-winning by teaching others to be soul-winners. Paul was a master in teaching Timothy and Titus and numerous others in the early church.

This writing effort is the result of my lifelong attempt to be a soul-winner. Special thanks to Mr. and Mrs. W. A. Ryan and Mr. and Mrs. J. W. Fisher who have been constant models to me. Loving dedication is to Judy, Jim, and Jeff—my family.

Bible Promises on God's Plan of Salvation

Am I Really a Sinner?

All we like a sheep have gone astray; we have turned every one to his own way; and the Lord hath laid on him the inquity of us all (Isa. 53:6).

For all have sinned, and come short of the glory of God (Rom. 3:23).

But the scripture hath concluded all under sin, that the promise by faith of Jesus Christ might be given to them that believe (Gal. 3:22).

There is none righteous, no, not one: There is none that understandeth, there is none that seeketh after God. They are all gone out of the way, they are together become unprofitable; there is none that doeth good, no, not one. Their throat is an open sepulchre; with their tongues they have used deceit; the poison of asps is under their lips: Whose mouth is full of cursing and bitterness: Their feet are swift to shed blood: Destruction and misery are in their ways: And the way of peace have they not known: There is no fear of God before their eyes (Rom. 3:10-18).

The Lord looked down from heaven upon the children of men, to see if there were any that did understand, and seek God. They are all gone aside, they are all together become filthy: there is none that doeth good, no, not one (Ps. 14:2-3).

If we say that we have no sin, we deceive ourselves, and the truth is not in us. If we say that we have not sinned, we make him a liar, and his word is not in us (1 John 1:8,10).

Wherefore, as by one man sin entered into the world, . . . for that all have sinned (Rom. 5:12).

For there is not a just man upon earth, that doeth good, and sinneth not (Eccl. 7:20).

Who can say, I have made my heart clean, I am pure from my sin? (Prov. 20:9).

What Are the Consequences of Sin?

For the wages of sin is death; but the gift of God is eternal life through Jesus Christ our Lord (Rom. 6:23).

You, that were sometime alienated and enemies in your mind by wicked works, yet now hath he reconciled (Col. 1:21).

Know ye not that the unrighteous shall not inherit the kingdom of God? (1 Cor. 6:9).

Now the works of the flesh are manifest, which are these; adultery, fornication, uncleanness, lasciviousness, idolatry, witchcraft, hatred, variance, emulations, wrath, strife, seditions, heresies, envyings, murders, drunkenness, revellings, and such like: of the which I tell you before, as I have also told you in time past, that they which do such things shall not inherit the kingdom of God (Gal. 5:19-21).

But the fearful, and unbelieving, and the abominable, and murderers and whoremongers, and sorcerers, and idolaters, and all liars, shall have their part in the lake which burneth with fire and brimstone: which is the second death (Rev. 21:8).

Wherefore, as by one man sin entered into the

world, and death by sin; and so death passed upon all men (Rom. 5:12).

Behold, all souls are mine; as the soul of the father, so also the soul of the son is mine: the soul that sinneth, it shall die (Ezek. 18:4).

For to be carnally minded is death; . . . Because the carnal mind is enmity against God: for it is not subject to the law of God, neither indeed can be. So then they that are in the flesh cannot please God (Rom. 8:6-8).

Woe to the wicked! it shall be ill with him: for the reward of his hands shall be given him (Isa. 3:11).

Does God Care About Me?

For God so loved the world, that he gave his only begotten Son, that whosoever believeth in him should not perish, but have everlasting life (John 3:16).

Herein is love, not that we loved God, but he loved us, and sent his Son to be the propitiation for our sins. Beloved, if God so loved us, we ought also to love one another (1 John 4:10-11).

For we ourselves also were sometimes foolish, disobedient, deceived, serving divers lusts and pleasures, living in malice and envy, hateful, and hating one another. But after that the kindness and love of God our Saviour toward man appeared (Titus 3:3-4).

The Father himself loveth you, because ye have loved me, and have believed that I came out from God (John 16:27).

Keep yourselves in the love of God, looking for the mercy of our Lord Jesus Christ unto eternal life (Jude 21).

God is love. . . . God sent his only begotten Son into the world, that we might live through him (1 John 4:8-9).

We love him, because he first loved us (1 John 4:19).

For I am persuaded, that neither death, nor life, nor angels, nor principalities, nor powers, nor things present, nor things to come, nor height, nor depth, nor any other creature, shall be able to separate us from the love of God, which is in Christ Jesus our Lord (Rom. 8:38-39).

Why Did God Send Jesus to Earth?

But as many as received him, to them gave he power to become the sons of God, even to them that believe on his name (John 1:12).

But God commendeth his love toward us, in that, while we were yet sinners, Christ died for us (Rom. 5:8).

For Christ also hath once suffered for sins, the just for the unjust, that he might bring us to God, being put to death in the flesh, but quickened by the Spirit (1 Pet. 3:18).

You, that were sometimes alienated and enemies in your mind by wicked works, yet now hath he reconciled in the body of his flesh through death, to present you holy and unblameable and unreproveable in his sight (Col. 1:21-22).

How much more shall the blood of Christ, who through the eternal Spirit offered himself without spot to God, purge your conscience from dead works to serve the living God? And for this cause he is the mediator of the new testament, that by means of death, for the redemption of the transgressions that were under the first testament, they which are called might receive the promise of eternal inheritance (Heb. 9:14-15).

God, who at sundry times and in divers manners spake in time past unto the fathers by the prophets, hath in these last days spoken unto us by his Son, whom he hath appointed heir of all things, by whom also he made the worlds; Who being the brightness of his glory, and the express image of his person, and upholding all things by the word of his power, when he had by himself purged our sins, sat down on the right hand of the Majesty on high (Heb. 1:1-3).

Walk in love, as Christ also hath loved us, and hath given himself for us (Eph. 5:2).

Neither is there salvation in any other: for there is none other name under heaven given among men, whereby we must be saved (Act 4:12).

The times of . . . ignorance God winked at; but now commandeth all men everywhere to repent: Because he hath appointed a day, in the which he will judge the world in righteousness by that man whom he hath ordained; whereof he hath given assurance unto all men, in that he hath raised him from the dead (Acts 17:30-31).

For the Son of man is not come to destroy men's lives, but to save them (Luke 9:56).

I am not come to call the righteous, but sinners to repentance (Matt. 9:13).

We have seen and do testify that the Father sent the Son to be the Saviour of the world. Whosoever shall confess that Jesus is the Son of God, God dwelleth in him, and he in God (1 John 4:14-15).

But where sin abounded, grace did much more abound: That as sin hath reigned unto death, even so might grace reign through righteousness unto eternal life by Jesus Christ our Lord (Rom. 5:20-21).

If any man sin, we have an advocate with the Father, Jesus Christ the righteous: And he is the propitiation for our sins: and not for ours only, but also for the sins of the whole world (1 John 2:1-2).

This is the record, that God hath given to us eternal life, and this life is in his Son (1 John 5:11).

Wherefore he is able also to save them to the uttermost that come unto God by him, seeing he ever liveth to make intercession for them (Heb. 7:25).

For he hath made him to be sin for us, who knew not sin; that we might be made the righteousness of God in him (2 Cor. 5:21).

What Am I to Do About Salvation?

Seek ye the Lord while he may be found, call ye upon him while he is near: Let the wicked forsake his way, and the unrighteous man his thoughts: and let him return unto the Lord, and he will have mercy upon him; and to our God, for he will abundantly pardon (Isa. 55:6-7).

Come now, and let us reason together, saith the Lord: though your sins be as scarlet, they shall be as white as snow; though they be red like crimson, they shall be as wool (Isa. 1:18).

The Spirit and the bride say, Come. And let him that heareth say, Come. And let him that is athirst come. And whosoever will, let him take the water of life freely (Rev. 22:17).

But whosoever drinketh of the water that I shall give him shall never thirst; but the water that I shall give him shall be in him a well of water springing up into everlasting life (John 4:14).

For to this end Christ both died, and rose, and revived, that he might be Lord both of the dead and living. For it is written, As I live, saith the Lord, every knee shall bow to me, and every tongue shall confess to God (Rom. 14:9,11).

He that covereth his sins shall not prosper: but whoso confesseth and forsaketh them shall have mercy (Prov. 28:13).

Blessed is he whose transgression is forgiven, whose sin is covered. Blessed is the man unto whom the Lord imputeth not iniquity. I acknowledged my sin unto thee, and mine iniquity have I not hid. I said, I will confess my transgressions unto the Lord; and thou forgavest the iniquity of my sin (Ps. 32:1-2,5).

To-day if ye will hear his voice, harden not your hearts (Heb. 3:15).

What Does God Offer Me?

Verily, Verily, I say unto you, He that believeth on me hath everlasting life (John 6:47).

Whosoever therefore shall confess me before men, him will I confess also before my Father which is in heaven (Matt. 10:32).

For Christ is the end of the law for righteousness to every one that believeth (Rom. 10:4).

Fight the good fight of faith, lay hold on eternal life, whereunto thou art also called, and hast professed a good profession before many witnesses. I give thee charge in the sight of God, who quickeneth all things (1 Tim. 6:12-13).

This is the promise that he hath promised us, even eternal life (1 John 2:25).

If we confess our sins, he is faithful and just to forgive us our sins, and to cleanse us from all unrighteousness (1 John 1:9).

I acknowledged my sin unto thee, and mine iniquity have I not hid. . . . I will confess my transgressions unto the Lord; and thou forgavest the iniquity of my sin (Ps. 32:5).

He that covereth his sins shall not prosper: but whoso confesseth and forsaketh them shall have mercy (Prov. 28:13).

There is therefore now no condemnation to them which are in Christ Jesus, who walk not after the flesh, but after the Spirit (Rom. 8:1).

Whosoever shall call upon the name of the Lord shall be saved (Rom. 10:13).

Sirs, what must I do to be saved? And they said, Believe on the Lord Jesus Christ, and thou shalt be saved (Acts 16:30-31).

Whosoever drinketh of the water that I shall give him shall never thirst; but the water that I shall give him shall be in him a well of water springing up into everlasting life (John 4:14).

He that hath the Son hath life; and he that hath not the Son of God hath not life (1 John 5:12).

What If I Refuse?

For God sent not his Son into the world to condemn the world; but that the world through him might be saved. He that believeth on him is not condemned: but He that believeth not is condemned already, because he hath not believed in the name of the only begotten Son of God (John 3:17-18).

There is no respect of persons with God. For as many as have sinned without law shall also perish without law: And as many as have sinned in the law shall be judged by the law (Rom. 2:11-12).

Then began he to upbraid the cities wherein most of his mighty works were done, because they repented not: Who unto thee, Chorazin! woe unto thee, Bethsaida! for if the mighty works, which were done in you, had been done in Tyre and Sidon, they would have repented long ago in sackcloth and ashes. But I say unto you, It shall be more tolerable for Tyre and Sidon at the day of judgment, than for you. And thou, Capernaum, which art exalted unto heaven, shalt be brought down to hell: for if the mighty works, which have been done in thee, had been done in Sodom, it would have remained until this day. But I say unto you, That it shall be more tolerable for the land of Sodom in the day of judgment, than for thee (Matt. 11:20-24).

What shall it profit a man, if he shall gain the whole world, and lose his own soul? Whosoever therefore shall be ashamed of me and of my words in this adulterous and sinful generation; of him also shall the Son of man be ashamed, when he cometh in the glory of his Father with the holy angels (Mark 8:36,38).

But whosoever shall deny me before men, him will I also deny before my Father which is in heaven (Matt. 10:33).

He that denieth me before men shall be denied before the angels of God (Luke 12:9).

I saw the dead, small and great, stand before God; and the books were opened: and another book was opened, which is the book of life: . . . And whosoever was not found written in the book of life was cast into the lake of fire (Rev. 20:12,15).

The fearful, and unbelieving, . . . shall have their part in the lake which burneth with fire and brimstone: which is the second death (Rev. 21:8).

Be not deceived; God is not mocked: for whatsoever a man soweth, that shall he also reap. For he that soweth to his flesh shall of the flesh reap corruption (Gal. 6:7-8).

Bible Promises to the Soul-winner

Soul-winning Is a Mandate from God

When I say unto the wicked, O wicked man, thou shalt surely die; if thou dost not speak to warn the wicked from his way, that wicked man shall die in his iniquity; but his blood will I require at thine hand. Nevertheless, if thou warn the wicked of his way to turn from it; if he do not turn from his way, he shall die in his iniquity; but thou hast delivered thy soul (Ezek. 33:8-9).

The fruit of the righteous is a tree of life; and he that winneth souls is wise (Prov. 11:30).

Though I preach the gospel, I have nothing to glory of: for necessity is laid upon me; yea, woe is unto me, if I preach not the gospel! (1 Cor. 9:16).

Look not every man on his own things, but every man also on the things of others (Phil. 2:4).

But ye shall receive power, after the Holy Ghost is come upon you: and ye shall be witnesses unto me both in Jerusalem, and in all Judea, and in Samaria, and unto the uttermost part of the earth (Acts 1:8).

Thus it is written, and thus it behoved Christ to suffer, and to rise from the dead the third day: And that repentance and remission of sins should be preached in his name among all nations, beginning at Jerusalem. And ye are witnesses of these things (Luke 24:46-48).

Let him know, that he which converteth the sinner from the error of his way, shall save a soul from death, and shall hide a multitude of sins (Jas. 5:20).

Keep yourselves in the love of God, looking for the mercy of our Lord Jesus Christ unto eternal life. And of some have compassion, making a difference: And others save with fear, pulling them out of the fire; hating even the garment spotted by the flesh (Jude 21-23).

Soul-winning Is a Partnership with God

Therefore we ought to give the more earnest heed to the things which we have heard, lest at any time we should let them slip. For if the word spoken by angels was steadfast, and every transgression and disobedience received a just recompence of reward; How shall we escape, if we neglect so great salvation; which at the first began to be spoken by the Lord, and was confirmed unto us by them that heard him (Heb. 2:1-3).

Therefore if any man be in Christ, he is a new creature: old things are passed away; behold, all things are become new. And all things are of God, who hath reconciled us to himself by Jesus Christ, and hath given to us the ministry of reconciliation; . . . and hath committed unto us the word of reconciliation. Now then we are ambassadors for Christ, as though God did beseech you by us: we pray you in Christ's stead, be ye reconciled to God (2 Cor. 5:17-20).

For it is God which worketh in you both to will and to do of his good pleasure (Phil. 2:13).

Therefore with joy shall ye draw water out of the wells of salvation. And . . . shall ye say, Praise the Lord, call upon his name, declare his doings among the people, make mention that his name is exalted (Isa. 12:3-4).

But ye are a chosen generation, a royal priesthood, an holy nation, a peculiar people; that ye should shew forth the praises of him who hath called you out of darkness into his marvellous light (1 Pet. 2:9).

Ye also, as lively stones, are built up a spiritual house, an holy priesthood, to offer up spiritual sacrifices, acceptable to God by Jesus Christ (1 Pet. 2:5).

Unto him that loved us, and washed us from our sins in his own blood, and hath made us kings and priests unto God and his Father; to him be glory and dominion for ever and ever. Amen (Rev. 1:5-6).

They sung a new song, saying, Thou are worthy to take the book, and to open the seals thereof: for thou was slain, and hast redeemed us to God by thy blood out of every kindred, and tongue, and people, and nation; and hast made us unto our God kings and priests: and we shall reign on the earth (Rev. 5:9-10).

Blessed and holy is he that hath part in the first resurrection: on such the second death hath no power, but they shall be priests of God and of Christ, and shall reign with him a thousand years (Rev. 20:6).

Soul-winning Is a Source of Great Joy

They that sow in tears shall reap in joy. He that goeth forth and weepeth, bearing precious seed, shall doubtless come again with rejoicing, bringing his sheaves with him (Ps. 126:5-6).

Many of them that sleep in the dust of the earth shall awake, some to everlasting life, and some to shame and everlasting contempt. And they that be wise shall shine as the brightness of the firmament; and they that turn many to righteousness as the stars for ever and ever (Dan. 12:2-3).

Cast thy bread upon the waters: for thou shalt find it after many days (Eccl. 11:1).

He turned him unto his disciples, and said privately, Blessed are the eyes which see the things that ye see: For I tell you, that many prophets and kings have desired to see those things which ye see, and have not seen them; and to hear those things which ye hear, and have not heard them (Luke 10:23-24).

The seventy returned again with joy, saying, Lord, even the devils are subject unto us through thy name (Luke 10:17).

He that reapeth receiveth wages, and gathereth fruit unto life eternal: that both he that soweth and he that reapeth may rejoice together (John 4:36).

Barnabas . . . who, when he came, and had seen the grace of God, was glad, and exhorted them all, that with purpose of heart they would cleave unto the Lord. For he was a good man, and full of the Holy Ghost and of faith: and much people was added unto the Lord (Acts 11:22-24).

I say unto you, that likewise joy shall be in heaven over one sinner that repenteth, more than over

ninety and nine just persons, which need no repentance (Luke 15:7).

Likewise, I say unto you there is joy in the presence of the angels of God over one sinner that repenteth (Luke 15:10).

It was meet that we should make merry, and be
glad: for this thy brother was dead, and is alive
again; and was lost, and is found (Luke 15:32).

Soul-winning Brings Great Rewards

Keep yourselves in the love of God, looking for
the mercy of our Lord Jesus Christ unto eternal life.
And of some have compassion, making a difference:
And others save with fear, pulling them out of the
fire; hating even the garment spotted by the flesh
(Jude 21-23). [Soul-winners use both compassion
and fear to bring people to Jesus Christ.]

I exhort therefore, that, first of all, supplications,
prayers, intercessions, and giving of thanks, be
made for all men; . . . For this is good and acceptable in the sight of God our Saviour; Who will have
all men to be saved, and to come unto the knowledge of the truth (1 Tim. 2:1,3-4). [Soul-winners
pray for the lost.]

Go ye therefore, and teach all nations, baptizing
them in the name of the Father, and of the Son, and
of the Holy Ghost: Teaching them to observe all
things whatsoever I have commanded you: and, lo,
I am with you alway, even unto the end of the world
(Matt. 28:19-20). [Soul-winners have the promise of
God's presence forever.]

Brethren, if any of you do err from the truth, and
one convert him; Let him know, that he which
converteth the sinner from the error of his way,

shall save a soul from death, and shall hide a multitude of sins (Jas. 5:19-20). [The soul-winner has saved a soul from death.]

The mouth of a righteous man is a well of life (Prov. 10:11).

The law of the wise is a fountain of life, to depart from the snares of death. . . . the way of transgressors is hard. . . . a fool layeth open his folly. A wicked messenger falleth into mischief: but a faithful ambassador is health (Prov. 13:14-17). [Soul-winners are faithful ambassadors who bring a fountain of life.]

His lord said unto him, Well done, thou good and faithful servant: thou hast been faithful over a few things, I will make thee ruler over many things: enter thou into the joy of thy lord (Matt. 25:21). [Soul-winners will know the joy of the Lord.]

He said unto him, Well, thou good servant: because thou hast been faithful in a very little, have thou authority over ten cities (Luke 19:17). [Soul-winners will rule with Jesus.]

Biblical Characteristics of the Soul-Winner

Soul-winners Know the Scripture

Study to shew thyself approved unto God, a workman that needeth not to be ashamed, rightly dividing the word of truth (2 Tim. 2:15).

A man of Ethiopia, an eunuch of great authority under Candace queen of the Ethiopians, . . . had come to Jerusalem for to worship, was returning, and sitting in his chariot read Esaias the prophet.

And Philip ran thither to him, . . . and said, Understandest thou what thou readest? And he said, How can I, except some man should guide me? Then Philip opened his mouth, and began at the same scripture, and preached unto him Jesus (Acts. 8:27-28,30-31,35).

Search the scriptures; for in them ye think ye have eternal life: and they are they which testify of me (John 5:39).

All scripture is given by inspiration of God, and is profitable for doctrine, for reproof, for correction, for instruction in righteousness: That the man of God may be perfect, throughly furnished unto all good works (2 Tim. 3:16-17).

They received the word with all readiness of mind, and searched the scriptures daily, whether those things were so (Acts 17:11).

Whatsoever things were written aforetime were written for our learning, that we through patience and comfort of the scripture might have hope (Rom. 15:4).

These things have I written unto you that believe on the name of the Son of God; that ye may know that ye have eternal life, and that ye may believe on the name of the Son of God (1 John 5:13).

Take the helmet of salvation, and the sword of the Spirit, which is the word of God (Eph. 6:17).

The word of God is quick, and powerful, and sharper than any two-edged sword, piercing even to the dividing asunder of soul and spirit, and of the joints and marrow, and is a discerner of the thoughts and intents of the heart (Heb. 4:12).

Let the word of Christ dwell in you richly in all wisdom (Col. 3:16).

Soul-winners Have the Mind of Christ

If there be therefore any consolation in Christ, if any comfort of love, if any fellowship of the Spirit, if any bowels and mercies, fulfil ye my joy, that ye be like-minded, having the same love, being of one accord, of one mind. Let this mind be in you, which was also in Christ Jesus (Phil. 2:1-2,5).

I have given you an example, that ye should do as I have done to you. . . . The servant is not greater than his lord; neither he that is sent greater than he that sent him. If ye know these things, happy are ye if ye do them (John 13:15-17).

Christ in you, the hope of glory: whom we preach, warning every man, and teaching every man in all wisdom; that we may present every man perfect in Christ Jesus (Col. 1:27-28).

When they saw the boldness of Peter and John, and perceived that they were unlearned and ignorant men, they marvelled; and they took knowledge of them, that they had been with Jesus (Acts 4:13).

God is faithful, by whom ye were called unto the fellowship of his Son Jesus Christ our Lord (1 Cor. 1:9).

I in them, and thou in me, that they may be made perfect in one; and that the world may know that thou hast sent me, and hast loved them, as thou hast loved me (John 17:23).

I am crucified with Christ: Nevertheless I live; yet not I, but Christ liveth in me: and the life which I now live in the flesh I live by the faith of the Son of God, who loved me, and gave himself for me (Gal. 2:20).

That Christ may dwell in your hearts by faith; that ye, being rooted and grounded in love, may be able to comprehend with all saints what is the breadth, and length, and depth, and height; And to know the love of Christ, which passeth knowledge (Eph. 3:17-19).

He that keepeth his commandments dwelleth in him, and he in him (1 John 3:24).

And if Christ be in you, the body is dead because of sin; but the Spirit is life because of righteousness (Rom. 8:10).

Soul-winners Are Filled with God's Spirit

Ye shall receive power, after that the Holy Ghost is come upon you: and ye shall be witnesses unto me both in Jerusalem, and in all Judea, and in Samaria, and unto the uttermost part of the earth (Acts. 1:8).

Be not drunk with wine, wherein is excess; but be filled with the Spirit (Eph. 5:18).

Then Peter, filled with the Holy Ghost, said unto them, Be it known unto you all, . . . that by the name of Jesus Christ of Nazareth, whom ye crucified, whom God raised from the dead, . . . This is the stone which . . . is become the head of the corner. Neither is there salvation in any other: for there is none other name under heaven given among men, whereby we must be saved (Acts 4:8,10-12).

Ananias went his way, and entered into the house; and putting his hands on him said, Brother Saul, the Lord, even Jesus, . . . hath sent me, that thou mightest receive thy sight, and be filled with the Holy Ghost. And immediately there fell from his eyes as it had been scales: and he received sight forthwith, and arose, and was baptized. And when he had received meat, he was strengthened. . . . And straightway he preached Christ in the synagogues, that he is the Son of God (Acts 9:17-20).

Hereby know we that we dwell in him, and he in us, because he hath given us of his Spirit (1 John 4:13).

Ye are not in the flesh, but in the Spirit, if so be that the Spirit of God dwell in you. But if the Spirit of him that raised up Jesus from the dead dwell in you, he that raised up Christ from the dead shall also quicken your mortal bodies by his Spirit that dwelleth in you (Rom. 8:9,11).

Even the Spirit of truth; whom the world cannot receive, because it seeth him not, neither knoweth him: but ye know him; for he dwelleth with you, and shall be in you (John 14:17).

What? know ye not that your body is the temple of the Holy Ghost which is in you, which ye have of God, and ye are not your own? (1 Cor. 6:19).

That good thing which was committed unto thee keep by the Holy Ghost which dwelleth in us (2 Tim. 1:14).

Soul-winners Love the Lost

Brethren, my heart's desire and prayer to God for Israel is, that they might be saved (Rom. 10:1).

I say the truth in Christ, I lie not, my conscience also bearing me witness in the Holy Ghost, That I have great heaviness and continual sorrow in my heart. For I could wish that myself were accursed from Christ for my brethren, my kinsmen according to the flesh (Rom. 9:1-3).

I am debtor both to the Greeks, and to the Barbarians; both to the wise, and to the unwise. So, as much as in me is, I am ready to preach the gospel to you that are at Rome also. For I am not ashamed of the gospel of Christ: for it is the power of God unto salvation to every one that believeth (Rom. 1:14-16).

Moses returned unto the Lord, and said, Oh, this people have sinned a great sin, . . . Yet now, if thou wilt forgive their sin—; and if not, blot me, I pray thee, out of thy book which thou hast written (Ex. 32:31-32).

If we love one another, God dwelleth in us, and his love is perfected in us. And we have seen and do testify that the Father sent the Son to be the Saviour of the world (1 John 4:12,14).

To the weak became I as weak, that I might gain the weak: I am made all things to all men, that I might by all means save some (1 Cor. 9:22).

Say not ye, There are yet four months, and then cometh harvest? behold, I say unto you, Lift up your eyes, and look on the fields; for they are white already to harvest (John 4:35).

If by any means I may provoke to emulation them which are my flesh, and might save some of them (Rom. 11:14). [Paul was concerned for the Jews.]

For the Son of man is come to save that which was lost (Matt. 18:11). [Jesus is our example in loving the lost.]

Soul-winners Are Faithful in Their Work

This is a faithful saying, and worthy of all acceptation, that Christ Jesus came into the world to save sinners; of whom I am chief. Howbeit for this cause I obtained mercy, that in me first Jesus Christ might shew forth all longsuffering, for a pattern to them which should hereafter believe on him to life everlasting (1 Tim. 1:15-16).

But by the grace of God I am what I am: and his grace which was bestowed upon me was not in vain; but I laboured more abundantly than they all: yet not I, but the grace of God which was with me (1 Cor. 15:10).

Then Paul stretched forth the hand, and answered for himself. Whereupon, O king Agrippa, I was not disobedient unto the heavenly vision: But shewed first unto them of Damascus, and at Jerusalem, and throughout all the coasts of Judaea, and then to the Gentiles, that they should repent and turn to God (Acts 26:1,19-20).

What doth it profit, my brethren, though a man say he hath faith, and have not works? can faith save him? Even so faith, if it hath not works, is dead, being alone. Yea, a man may say, Thou hast faith, and I have works: shew me thy faith without thy works, and I will shew thee my faith by my works (Jas. 2:14,17-18).

I am set for the defence of the gospel. Only let your conversation be as it becometh the gospel of Christ: that whether I come and see you, or else be absent, I may hear of your affairs, that ye stand fast in one spirit, with one mind striving together for the faith of the gospel (Phil. 1:17,27).

Others save with fear, pulling them out of the fire; hating even the garment spotted by the flesh (Jude 23).

Therefore, my beloved brethren, be ye steadfast, unmoveable, always abounding in the work of the Lord, forasmuch as ye know that your labour is not in vain in the Lord (1 Cor. 15:58).

For God is not unrighteous to forget your work

and labour of love, which ye have shewed toward his name (Heb. 6:10).

They that be wise shall shine as the brightness of the firmament; and they that turn many to righteousness as the stars for ever and ever (Dan. 12:3).

Soul-winners Are Watchful

Go ye therefore into the highways, and as many as ye shall find, bid to the marriage (Matt. 22:9). [Soul-winners are to seek everywhere.]

Then cometh he to a city of Samaria, which is called Sychar, near to the parcel of ground that Jacob gave to his son Joseph. Now Jacob's well was there. . . . There cometh a woman of Samaria to draw water: Jesus saith unto her, Give me to drink (John 4:5-7). [Jesus sought to win this woman.]

Wherefore he saith, Awake thou that sleepest, and arise from the dead, and Christ shall give thee light. See then that ye walk circumspectly, not as fools, but as wise, redeeming the time; because the days are evil (Eph. 5:14-16). [Soul-winners are to use time wisely.]

Walk in wisdom toward them that are without, redeeming the time (Col. 4:5).

Dearly beloved, I beseech you as strangers and pilgrims, abstain from fleshly lusts, which war against the soul; Having your conversation honest among the Gentiles: that, whereas they speak against you as evildoers, they may by your good works, which they shall behold, glorify God in the day of visitation (1 Pet. 2:11-12). [Soul-winners are to give a witness by their lives.]

Then shall the righteous shine forth as the sun in

the kingdom of their Father (Matt. 13:43). [Righteous people are to shrine.]

Let your light so shine before men, that they may see your good works, and glorify your Father which is in heaven (Matt. 5:16).

Herein is my Father glorified, that ye bear much fruit; so shall ye be my disciples (John 15:8).

That ye might walk worthy of the Lord unto all pleasing, being fruitful in every good work, and increasing in the knowledge of God (Col. 1:10).

In all things shewing thyself a pattern of good works: in doctrine shewing uncorruptness, gravity, sincerity (Titus 2:7). [Soul-winners are to set a pattern for others to imitate.]

Therefore watch, and remember, that by the space of three years I ceased not to warn every one night and day with tears (Acts 20:31).

Bible Preparation for Soul-winning

Conviction that People Are Lost

Have mercy upon me, O God, according to thy lovingkindness: according unto the multitude of thy tender mercies blot out my transgressions. Wash me thoroughly from mine iniquity, and cleanse me from my sin. For I acknowledge my transgressions: and my sin is ever before me. Against thee, thee only, have I sinned, . . . Behold, I was shapen in iniquity, and in sin did my mother conceive me (Ps. 51:1-5).

For if God spared not the angels that sinned, but cast them down to hell, and delivered them into chains of darkness, to be reserved unto judgment; and spared not the old world, . . . and turning the cities of Sodom and Gomorrha into ashes condemned them with an overthrow, making them an ensample unto those that after should live ungodly. The Lord knoweth how to . . . reserve the unjust unto the day of judgment to be punished (2 Pet. 2:4-6,9).

He that believeth not the Son shall not see life; but the wrath of God abideth on him (John 3:36).

Now the works of the flesh are . . . these; Adultery, fornication, uncleanness, lasciviousness, idolatry, witchcraft, hatred, variance, emulations, wrath, strife, seditions, heresies, envyings, murders, drunkenness, revellings, . . . they which do such things shall not inherit the kingdom of God (Gal. 5:19-21).

All we like sheep have gone astray; we have turned every one to his own way; and the Lord hath laid on him the iniquity of us all (Isa. 53:6).

I said therefore unto you, that ye shall die in your sins: for if ye believe not that I am he, ye shall die in your sins (John 8:24). [Jesus' statement to unbelieving Jews.]

Therefore as by the offence of one judgment came upon all men to condemnation; (Rom. 5:18).

Be not deceived; God is not mocked: for whatsoever a man soweth, that shall he also reap. For he that soweth to his flesh shall of the flesh reap corruption (Gal. 6:7-8).

For the wages of sin is death (Rom. 6:23).

Concern for the Spiritual Welfare of Lost Persons

Andrew, Simon Peter's brother. He first findeth his own brother Simon, and saith unto him, We have found the Messias, which is, being interpreted, the Christ. And he brought him to Jesus (John 1:40-42).

Philip findeth Nathanael, and saith unto him, We have found him, of whom Moses in the law, and the prophets, did write, Jesus of Nazareth (John 1:45).

There was a certain rich man, . . . the rich man also died, and was buried; And in hell he lift up his eyes, being in torments, and seeth Abraham afar off, and Lazarus in his bosom. Then he said, I pray thee therefore, father, that thou wouldest send him to my father's house: For I have five brethren; that he may testify unto them, lest they also come into this place of torment (Luke 16:19,22-23,27-28).

Brethren, my heart's desire and prayer to God for Israel is, that they might be saved (Rom. 10:1).

To the weak became I as weak, that I might gain the weak: I am made all things to all men, that I might by all means save some (1 Cor. 9:22).

If by any means I may provoke to emulation them which are my flesh, and might save some of them (Rom. 11:14).

Say not ye, there are yet four months, and then cometh harvest? behold, I say unto you, Lift up your eyes, and look on the fields; for they are white already to harvest (John 4:35).

For I could wish that myself were accursed from Christ for my brethren, my kinsmen according to the flesh (Rom. 9:3).

Confidence in Him Who Is Able to Forgive and Save

Come now, and let us reason together, saith the Lord: though your sins be as scarlet, they shall be as white as snow; though they be red like crimson, they shall be as wool (Isa. 1:18).

Wherefore he is able also to save them to the uttermost that come unto God by him, seeing he ever liveth to make intercession for them (Heb. 7:25).

She shall bring forth a son, and thou shalt call his name Jesus: for he shall save his people from their sins (Matt. 1:21).

And if any man hear my words, and believe not, I judge him not, for I came not to judge the world, but to save the world (John 12:47).

This is a faithful saying, and worthy of all acceptation, that Christ Jesus came into the world to save sinners; of whom I am chief (1 Tim. 1:15).

For the Son of man is come to seek and to save that which was lost (Luke 19:10).

The Lord is not slack concerning his promise, as some men count slackness; but is longsuffering to us-ward, not willing that any should perish, but that all should come to repentance (2 Pet. 3:9).

Grace and peace be multiplied unto you through the knowledge of God, and of Jesus our Lord, according as his divine power hath given unto us all things that pertain unto life and godliness (2 Pet. 1:2-3).

But God, who is rich in mercy, for his great love wherewith he loved us, even when we were dead in sins, hath quickened us together with Christ, (by grace ye are saved) (Eph. 2:4-5).

A new heart also will I give you, and a new spirit will I put within you: and I will take away the stony heart out of your flesh, and I will give you an heart of flesh (Ezek. 36:26).

If thou canst believe, all things are possible to him that believeth (Mark 9:23).

Now unto him that is able to keep you from falling, and to present you faultless before the presence of his glory with exceeding joy (Jude 24).

Now unto him that is able to do exceeding abundantly above all that we ask or think, according to the power that worketh in us (Eph. 3:20).

Continuation in Desire and Effort

Let us not be weary in well-doing: for in due season we shall reap, if we faint now (Gal. 6:9).

As the Father hath loved me, so have I loved you: continue ye in my love (John 15:9).

Behold, I come quickly: hold that fast which thou hast, that no man take thy crown (Rev. 3:11).

But continue thou in the things which thou hast learned and hast been assured of, knowing of whom thou hast learned them (2 Tim. 3:14).

Therefore said he unto them, The harvest truly is great, but the labourers are few: pray ye therefore the Lord of the harvest, that he would send forth labourers into his harvest (Luke 10:2).

Say not ye, There are yet four months, and then cometh harvest? behold, I say unto you, Lift up your eyes, and look on the fields; for they are white already to harvest. And he that reapeth receiveth wages, and gathereth fruit unto life eternal: that both he that soweth and he that reapeth may rejoice together (John 4:35-36).

Therefore, my beloved brethren, be ye steadfast, unmoveable, always abounding in the work of the Lord, forasmuch as ye know that your labour is not in vain in the Lord (1 Cor. 15:58).

Not by works of righteousness which we have done, but according to his mercy he saved us, . . . That being justified by his grace, we should be made heirs according to the hope of eternal life. This is a faithful saying, and these things I will that thou affirm constantly (Titus 3:5,7-8).

Preach the word; be instant in season, out of season; reprove, rebuke, exhort with all longsuffering and doctrine (2 Tim. 4:2).

Blessed are they which do hunger and thirst after righteousness: for they shall be filled (Matt. 5:6).

Exhort one another daily, while it is called To-day; lest any of you be hardened through the deceitfulness of sin (Heb. 3:13).

For we cannot but speak the things which we have seen and heard (Acts 4:20).

Consecration in Daily Living

He saith unto them, Follow me, and I will make you fishers of men. (Matt. 4:19).

I beseech you therefore, brethren, by the mercies of God, that ye present your bodies a living sacrifice, holy, acceptable unto God, which is your reasonable service. And be not conformed to this world: but be ye transformed by the renewing of your mind, that ye may prove what is that good, and acceptable, and perfect, will of God (Rom. 12:1-2).

Ye are the temple of the living God; as God hath said, . . . I will be their God, and they shall be my people. Wherefore come out from among them, and be ye separate, saith the Lord (2 Cor. 6:16).

Love not the world, neither the things that are in the world. The world passeth away, . . . but he that doeth the will of God abideth forever (1 John 2:15, 17).

Wherefore seeing we also are compassed about with so great a cloud of witnesses, let us lay aside every weight, and the sin which doth so easily beset us, and let us run with patience the race that is set before us (Heb. 12:1).

For none of us liveth to himself. We live unto the Lord. It is good neither to eat flesh, nor to drink wine, nor any thing whereby thy brother stumbleth, or is offended, or is made weak (Rom. 14:7,8,21).

But what things were gain to me, those I counted loss for Christ. Yea, doubtless, and I count all things but loss for the excellency of the knowledge of Christ Jesus my Lord: for whom I have suffered the loss of all things, and do count them but dung, that I may win Christ (Phil. 3:7-8).

Whoso looketh into the perfect law of liberty, and continueth therein, he being not a forgetful hearer, but a doer of the work, this man shall be blessed in his deed (Jas. 1:25).

Whatsoever we ask, we receive of him, because we keep his commandments, and do those things that are pleasing in his sight (1 John 3:22).

Ye are the light of the world. Let your light so shine before men, that they may see your good works, and glorify your father which is in heaven (Matt. 5:14,16).

Therefore to him that knoweth to do good, and doeth it not, to him it is sin (Jas. 4:17).

Commitment to Prayer

Brethren, my heart's desire and prayer to God for Israel is, that they might be saved (Rom. 10:1).

The effectual fervent prayer of a righteous man availeth much (Jas. 5:16).

Again I say unto you, That if two of you shall agree on earth as touching any thing that they shall ask, it shall be done for them of my Father which is in heaven (Matt. 18:19).

It came to pass . . . that Moses said unto the people, Ye have sinned a great sin: and now I will go up unto the Lord; . . . And Moses returned unto the Lord, and said, Oh, this people have sinned a great sin, . . . Yet now, if thou wilt forgive their sin—; and if not, blot me, I pray thee, out of thy book which thou hast written (Ex. 32:30-32).

If ye abide in me, and my words abide in you, ye shall ask what ye will, and it shall be done unto you (John 15:7).

He spake a parable unto them to this end, that men ought always to pray, and not to faint (Luke 18:1).

Praying always with all prayer and supplication in the Spirit, and watching thereunto with all perseverance and supplication for all saints (Eph. 6:18).

Pray without ceasing (1 Thess. 5:17).

Continue in prayer (Col. 4:2).

Be careful for nothing; but in every thing by prayer and supplication with thanksgiving let your requests be made known unto God (Phil. 4:6).

I will therefore that men pray every where, lifting up holy hands, without wrath and doubting (1 Tim. 2:8).

This is the confidence that we have in him, that,

if we ask any thing according to his will, he heareth us. And if we know that he hear us, whatsoever we ask, we know that we have the petitions that we desired of him (1 John 5:14-15).

Courage to Approach the Unsaved

Behold, I send you forth as sheep in the midst of wolves: be ye therefore wise as serpents, and harmless as doves. But when they deliver you up, take no thought how or what ye shall speak: for it shall be given you in that same hour what ye shall speak. For it is not ye that speak, but the Spirit of your Father which speaketh in you (Matt. 10:16,19-20).

For I will give you a mouth and wisdom, which all your adversaries shall not be able to gainsay nor resist (Luke 21:15).

Which things also we speak, not in the words which man's wisdom teacheth, but which the Holy Ghost teacheth; comparing spiritual things with spiritual (1 Cor. 2:13).

Now therefore go, and I will be with thy mouth, and teach thee what thou shalt say (Ex. 4:12). [God commanding Moses to be courageous.]

The Lord hath given me the tongue of the learned, that I should know how to speak a word in season to him that is weary (Isa. 50:4). [God's promise to Isaiah].

Apollos, . . . an eloquent man, and mighty in the scriptures, came to Ephesus. This man was instructed in the way of the Lord; and being fervent in the spirit, he spake and taught diligently the things of the Lord, knowing only the baptism of John. And he began to speak boldly in the synagogue: whom when Aquila and Priscilla had heard, they took him unto them, and expounded unto him the way of God more perfectly (Acts 18:24-26).

Now when they saw the boldness of Peter and John, and perceived that they were unlearned and ignorant men, they marvelled; and they took knowledge of them, that they had been with Jesus (Acts 4:13).

When they had prayed, the place was shaken where they were assembled together; and they were all filled with the Holy Ghost, and they spake the word of God with boldness (Acts 4:31).

Watch ye, stand fast in the faith, quit you like men, be strong (1 Cor. 16:13).

Finally, my brethren, be strong in the Lord, and in the power of his might. Put on the whole armour of God, that ye may be able to stand against the wiles of the devil (Eph. 6:10-11).

Thou therefore, my son, be strong in the grace that is in Christ Jesus. And the things that thou hast heard of me among many witnesses, the same commit thou to faithful men, who shall be able to teach others also (2 Tim. 2:1-2).

Barnabas took him [Paul], and brought him to the apostles, and declared unto them . . . how he had preached boldly at Damascus in the name of Jesus. And he was with them coming in and going out at Jerusalem. And he spake boldly in the name of the Lord Jesus (Acts 9:27-29).

Bible Promises to the Lost

You Can Have Faith in God's Word

If we believe not, yet he abideth faithful: he cannot deny himself (2 Tim. 2:13).

Every good gift and every perfect gift is from above, and cometh down from the Father of lights, with whom is no variableness, neither shadow of turning (Jas. 1:17).

But thou [God] art the same, and thy years shall have no end (Ps. 102:27).

For I am the Lord, I change not; therefore ye sons of Jacob are not consumed (Mal. 3:6).

Jesus Christ the same yesterday, and to-day, and for ever (Heb. 13:8).

It is written, Man shall not live by bread alone, but by every word that proceedeth out of the mouth of God (Matt. 4:4).

For verily I say unto you, Till heaven and earth pass, one jot or one tittle shall in no wise pass from the law, till all be fulfilled (Matt. 5:18). [God's Word is sure.]

For I am the Lord; I will speak, and the word that I shall speak shall come to pass (Ezek. 12:25).

Heaven and earth shall pass away: but my words shall not pass away (Luke 21:33).

God is faithful, by whom ye were called unto the fellowship of his Son Jesus Christ our Lord (1 Cor. 1:9).

That by two immutable things, in which it was impossible for God to lie, we might have a strong consolation, who have fled for refuge to lay hold upon the hope set before us (Heb. 6:18).

You Can Have Faith in God's Work

Moreover, brethren, I declare unto you the gospel which I preached unto you, which also ye have received, and wherein ye stand; By which also, ye are saved, if he keep in memory what I preached unto you, unless ye have believed in vain. For I delivered unto you first of all that which I also received, now that Christ died for our sins according to the scriptures (1 Cor. 15:1-3).

For we are his workmanship, created in Christ Jesus unto good works, which God hath before ordained that we should walk in them (Eph. 2:10).

Beware lest any man spoil you through philosophy and vain deceit, after the tradition of men, after the rudiments of the world, and not after Christ. For in him dwelleth all the fulness of the Godhead bodily, and ye are complete in him, which is the head of all principality and power. (Col. 2:8-10).

Without controversy great is the mystery of godliness: God was manifest in the flesh, justified in the Spirit, seen of angels, preached unto the Gentiles, believed on in the world, received up into glory (1 Tim. 3:16).

Being confident of this very thing, that he which hath begun a good work in you will perform it until the day of Jesus Christ (Phil. 1:6).

You Can Have Faith in God's Will

If any man will do his will, he shall know of the doctrine, whether it be of God, or whether I speak of myself (John 7:17).

We know that all things work together for good

to them that love God, to them who are called according to his purpose (Rom. 8:28).

Now the God of peace, that brought again from the dead our Lord Jesus, that great shepherd of the sheep, through the blood of the everlasting covenant, make you perfect in every good work to do his will, working in you that which is well-pleasing in his sight, through Jesus Christ; to whom be glory for ever and every (Heb. 13:20-21).

For that ye ought to say, If the Lord will, we shall live, and do this, or that (Jas. 4:15).

The world passeth away, and the lust thereof: but he that doeth the will of God abideth for ever (1 John 2:17).

You Can Have Faith in God's Wonder

For unto us a child is born, unto us a son is given: and the government shall be upon his shoulder: and his name shall be called Wonderful, Counsellor, The mighty God, The everlasting Father, The Prince of Peace, of the increase of his government and peace there shall be no end, . . . The zeal of the Lord of hosts will perform this (Isa. 9:6-7).

Thou shalt call his name Jesus: for he shall save his people from their sins (Matt. 1:21).

Wherefore God also hath highly exalted him, and given him a name which is above every name: That at the name of Jesus every knee should bow, of things in heaven, and things in earth, and things under the earth; And that every tongue should confess that Jesus Christ is Lord, to the glory of God the Father (Phil. 2:9-11).

He hath on his vesture and on his thigh a name

written, King of kings, and Lord of lords (Rev. 19:16).

Wherefore God also hath highly exalted him, and given him a name which is above every name: That at the name of Jesus every knee should bow, of things in heaven, and things in earth, and things under the earth (Phil. 2:9-10).

For after that in the wisdom of God the world by wisdom knew not God, it pleased God by the foolishness of preaching to save them that believe (1 Cor. 1:21).

You Can Have Faith in God's Wisdom

Because the foolishness of God is wiser than men; and the weakness of God is stronger than men (1 Cor. 1:25).

O the depth of the riches both of the wisdom and knowledge of God! how unsearchable are his judgments, and his ways past finding out! (Rom. 11:33).

Christ; In whom are hid all the treasures of wisdom and knowledge (Col. 2:2-3).

If any of you lack wisdom, let him ask of God, that giveth to all men liberally, and upbraideth not; and it shall be given him (Jas. 1:5).

For if our heart condemn us, God is greater than our heart, and knoweth all things (1 John 3:20).

Bible Answers for Excuses

"I Like My Life Just as It Is"

One thing thou lackest: go thy way, sell whatsoever thou hast, and give to the poor, and thou shalt have treasure in heaven: and come, take up the cross, and follow me (Mark 10:21). [This was Jesus' answer to a man who claimed to have kept God's Commandments from his youth.]

Know ye not that the friendship of the world is enmity with God? whosoever therefore will be a friend of the world is the enemy of God (Jas. 4:4). [God demands total surrender to His will and way.]

The world passeth away, and the lust thereof: but he that doeth the will of God abideth for ever (1 John 2:17). [The person who surrenders to God's will abides forever.]

Be not deceived; God is not mocked: for whatsoever a man soweth, that shall he also reap. For he that soweth to his flesh shall of the flesh reap corruption; but he that soweth to the Spirit shall of the Spirit reap life everlasting (Gal. 6:7-8). [The person who surrenders to God's will shall have everlasting life.]

How shall we escape, if we neglect so great salvation; which at the first began to be spoken by the Lord, and was confirmed unto us by them that heard him (Heb. 2:3). [There is no escape from God.]

Fear not them which kill the body, but are not able to kill the soul: but rather fear him which is able to destroy both soul and body in hell (Matt. 10:28). [Jesus said we should fear God who has power over body and soul.]

Be not highminded, but fear: For if God spared not the natural branches, take heed lest he also spare not thee. Behold therefore the goodness and severity of God (Rom. 11:20-22). [God is good, but those who choose their own way and reject His plan shall be cut off.]

"Others Are Worse than Me"

I saw the dead, small and great, stand before God; and the books were opened: and another book was opened, which is the book of life: And whosoever was not found written in the book of life was cast into the lake of fire (Rev. 20:12,15).

So then every one of us shall give account of himself to God (Rom. 14:12).

Therefore is the kingdom of heaven likened unto a certain king, which would take account of his servants (Matt. 18:23). [God judges each of us individually.]

For every one that exalteth himself shall be abased; and he that humbleth himself shall be exalted (Luke 18:14).

Whosoever shall exalt himself shall be abased; and he that shall humble himself shall be exalted (Matt. 23:12).

For they being ignorant of God's righteousness, and going about to establish their own righteousness, have not submitted themselves unto the righteousness of God (Rom. 10:3).

The way of a fool is right in his own eyes: but he that hearkeneth unto counsel is wise (Prov. 12:15).

Most men will proclaim every one his own goodness: but a faithful man who can find? (Prov. 20:6).

There is a generation that are pure in their own

eyes, and yet is not washed from their filthiness (Prov. 30:12).

Yet thou sayest, Because I am innocent, surely his anger shall turn from me. Behold, I will plead with thee, because thou sayest, I have not sinned (Jer. 2:35).

For we dare not make ourselves of the number, or compare ourselves with some that commend themselves: but they measuring themselves by themselves, and comparing themselves among themselves, are not wise (2 Cor. 10:12).

Therefore to him that knoweth to do good, and doeth it not, to him it is sin (Jas. 4:17).

"The Church Is Full of Hypocrites"

Therefore thou art inexcusable, O man, whosoever thou art that judgest: for wherein thou judgest another, thou condemnest thyself; for thou that judgest doest the same things (Rom. 2:1).

Who are thou that judgest another man's servant? to his own master he standeth or faileth. Yea, he shall be holden up: for God is able to make him stand (Rom. 14:4).

Every one of us shall give account of himself to God. Let us not therefore judge one another any more: but judge this rather, that no man put a stumblingblock or an occasion to fall in his brother's way (Rom. 14:12-13).

I know nothing by myself; yet am I not hereby justified: but he that judgeth me is the Lord. Therefore judge nothing before the time, until the Lord come, who both will bring to light the hidden things of darkness, and will make manifest the counsels of the hearts: and then shall every man have praise of God (1 Cor. 4:4-5).

There is one lawgiver, who is able to save and to destroy: who art thou that judgest another? (Jas. 4:12).

Judge not, that ye be not judged. For with what judgment ye judge, ye shall be judged: and with what measure ye measure, it shall be measured to you again. And why beholdest thou the mote that is in thy brother's eye, but considerest not the beam that is in thine own eye? Thou hypocrite, first cast out the beam out of thine own eye; and then shalt thou see clearly to cast out the mote out of thy brother's eye (Matt. 7:1-3,5).

He hath shewed the, O man, what is good; and what doth the Lord require of thee, but to do justly, and to love mercy, and to walk humbly with thy God? (Mic. 6:8).

"When I Clean Up My Life"

Jesus answered and said unto him, Verily, verily, I say unto thee, Except a man be born again, he cannot see the kingdom of God (John 3:3).

This is the record, that God hath given to us eternal life, and this life is in his Son. He that hath the Son hath life; and he that hath not the Son of God hath not life. These things have I written unto you that believe on the name of the Son of God; that ye may know that ye have eternal life, and that ye may believe on the name of the Son of God. And this is the confidence that we have in him, that, if we ask anything according to his will, he heareth us (1 John 5:11-14).

For by grace are ye saved through faith; and that

not of yourselves: it is the gift of God: Not of works, lest any man should boast (Eph. 2:8-9).

This is a faithful saying, and worthy of all acceptation, that Christ Jesus came into the world to save sinners; of whom I am chief (1 Tim. 1:15).

Therefore, if any man be in Christ, he is a new creature: old things are passed away; behold, all things are become new (2 Cor. 5:17).

For I the Lord thy God will hold thy right hand, saying unto thee, Fear not; I will help thee (Isa. 41:13).

That which I do I allow not: for what I would, that do I not; but what I hate, that do I. If then I do that which I would not, I consent unto the law that it is good. Now then it is no more I that do it, but sin that dwelleth in me. For I know that in me (that is, in my flesh), dwelleth no good thing: for to will is present with me; but how to perform that which is good I find not. For the good that I would I do not: but the evil which I would not, that I do (Rom. 7:15-19). [Men and women need God's help to do the right thing.]

If we confess our sins, he is faithful and just to forgive us our sins, and to cleanse us from all unrighteousness (1 John 1:9).

"God Is Too Good to Send Me to Hell"

He that believeth on the Son hath everlasting life: and he that believeth not the Son shall not see life; but the wrath of God abideth on him (John 3:36).

For the wrath of God is revealed from heaven against all ungodliness and unrighteousness of men, who hold the truth in unrighteousness (Rom. 1:18).

Let no man deceive you with vain words: for

because of these things cometh the wrath of God upon the children of disobedience (Eph. 5:6).

Know ye not the unrighteous shall not inherit the kingdom of God? Be not deceived: neither fornicators, nor idolaters, nor adulterers, nor effeminate, nor abusers of themselves with mankind, nor thieves, nor covetous, nor drunkards, nor revilers, nor extortioners, shall inherit the kingdom of God (1 Cor. 6:9-10).

And every one that heareth these sayings of mine, and doeth them not, shall be likened unto a foolish man, which built his house upon the sand: And the rain descended, and the floods came, and the winds blew, and beat upon that house; and it fell: and great was the fall of it (Matt. 7:26-27).

I saw the dead, small and great, stand before God; and the books were opened: and another book was opened, which is the book of life: And whosoever was not found written in the book of life was cast into the lake of fire (Rev. 20:12,15).

But the fearful, and unbelieving, . . . shall have their part in the lake which burneth with fire and brimstone: which is the second death (Rev. 21:8).

He that rejecteth me, and receiveth not my words, hath one that judgeth him: the word that I have spoken, the same shall judge him in the last day (John 12:48).

To you who are troubled rest with us, when the Lord Jesus shall be revealed from heaven with his mighty angels, in flaming fire taking vengeance on them that know not God, and that obey not the gospel of our Lord Jesus Christ (2 Thess. 1:7-8).

For we know him that hath said, Vengeance belongeth unto me, I will recompense, saith the Lord. And again, The Lord shall judge his people. It is a fearful thing to fall into the hands of the living God (Heb. 10:30-31).

"I Live a Good Life"

We know that the Son of God is come, and hath given us an understanding, that we may know him that is true, and we are in him that is true, even in his Son Jesus Christ. This is the true God, and eternal life (1 John 5:20).

Many will say to me in that day, Lord, Lord, have we not prophesied in thy name? and in thy name have cast out devils? and in thy name done many wonderful works? And then will I profess unto them, I never knew you: depart from me, ye that work iniquity (Matt. 7:22-23).

Therefore by the deeds of the law there shall no flesh be justified in his sight: for by the law is the knowledge of sin (Rom. 3:20).

Knowing that a man is not justified by the works of the law, but by the faith of Jesus Christ, even we have believed in Jesus Christ, that we might be justified by the faith of Christ, and not by the works of the law: for by the works of the law shall no flesh be justified (Gal. 2:16).

For by grace are ye saved through faith; and that not of yourselves: it is the gift of God: Not of works, lest any man should boast (Eph. 2:8-9).

But after that the kindness and love of God our Saviour toward man appeared, not by works of righteousness which we have done, but according to his mercy he saved us, by the washing of regeneration, and renewing of the Holy Ghost (Titus 3:4-5).

Jesus . . . said . . . Verily, verily, I say unto thee,

Except a man be born again, he cannot see the kingdom of God (John 3:3).

Who his own self bare our sins in his own body on the tree, that we, being dead to sins, should live unto righteousness: by whose stripes ye were healed. For ye were as sheep going astray; but are now returned unto the Shepherd and Bishop of your souls (1 Pet. 2:24-25).

But the scripture hath concluded all under sin, that the promise by faith of Jesus Christ might be given to them that believe (Gal. 3:22).

"I Do Not Believe in Hell"

There was certain rich man, which was clothed in purple and fine linen, and fared sumptuously every day: . . . the rich man also died, . . . And in hell he lift up his eyes, being in torments, . . . And he cried and said, Father Abraham, have mercy on me, and send Lazarus, that he may dip the tip of his finger in water, and cool my tongue; for I am tormented in this flame (Luke 16:19,22-24).

Then shall he say also unto them on the left hand, Depart from me, ye cursed, into everlasting fire, prepared for the devil and his angels (Matt. 25:41).

If thy hand offend thee, cut it off: it is better for thee to enter into life maimed, than having two hands to go into hell, into the fire that never shall be quenched: Where their worm dieth not, and the fire is not quenched (Mark 9:43-44).

If our gospel be hid, it is hid to them that are lost: In whom the god of this world hath blinded the minds of them which believe not, lest the light of the glorious gospel of Christ, who is the image of God, should shine unto them (2 Cor. 4:3-4). [Satan blinds those who do not believe in hell.]

To you who are troubled rest with us, when the Lord Jesus shall be revealed from heaven with his mighty angels, in flaming fire taking vengeance on them that know not God, and that obey not the gospel of our Lord Jesus Christ: Who shall be punished with everlasting destruction from the presence of the Lord, and from the glory of his power (2 Thess. 1:7-9).

The Lord knoweth how to deliver the godly out of temptations, and to reserve the unjust unto the day of judgment to be punished (2 Pet. 2:9).

If any man worship the beast and his image, and receive his mark in his forehead, or in his hand, the same shall drink of the wine of the wrath of God, . . . and he shall be tormented with fire and brimstone . . . And the smoke of their torment ascendeth up for ever and ever (Rev. 14:9-11).

But the fearful, and unbelieving, and the abominable, and murderers, and whoremongers, and sorcerers, and idolaters, and all liars, shall have their part in the lake which burneth with fire and brimstone: which is the second death (Rev. 21:8).

The Son of man shall send forth his angels, and they shall gather out of his kingdom all things that offend, and them which do iniquity; And shall cast them into a furnace of fire: there shall be wailing and gnashing of teeth (Matt. 13:41-42).

And if thine eye offend thee, pluck it out, and cast it from thee: it is better for thee to enter into life with one eye, rather than having two eyes to be cast into hell fire (Matt. 18:9).

"I Am Not Ready"

(For he saith, I have heard thee in a time accepted, and in the day of salvation have I succoured thee: behold, now is the accepted time; behold, now is the day of salvation.) (2 Cor. 6:2).

No man can serve two masters: for either he will hate the one, and love the other; or else he will hold to the one, and despise the other. Ye cannot serve God and mammon. But seek ye first the kingdom of God, and his righteousness; and all these things shall be added unto you (Matt. 6:24,33).

But as for me, my prayer is unto thee, O Lord, in an acceptable time: O God, in the multitude of thy mercy hear me, in the truth of thy salvation (Ps. 69:13).

He is our God; and we are the people of his pasture, and the sheep of his hand. To-day if ye will hear his voice, harden not your heart (Ps. 95:7-8).

Thus saith the Lord, In an acceptable time have I heard thee, and in a day of salvation have I helped thee (Isa. 49:8). [God has His accepted time, His timetable.]

Sow to yourselves in righteousness, reap in mercy; break up your fallow ground: for it is time to seek the Lord, till he come and rain righteousness upon you (Hos. 10:12).

For thus saith the Lord unto the house of Israel, Seek ye me, and ye shall live (Amos 5:4).

Seek ye the Lord, all ye meek of the earth, which have wrought his judgment; seek righteousness, seek meekness: it may be ye shall be hid in the day of the Lord's anger (Zeph. 2:3).

"When I Have the Feeling"

Behold, I stand at the door, and knock: if any man hear my voice, and open the door, I will come in to him, and will sup with him, and he with me (Rev. 3:20). [Jesus will come into your heart anytime you open it.]

It shall come to pass, that whosoever shall call on the name of the Lord shall be saved (Acts 2:21).

As many as received him, to them gave he power to become the sons of God, even to them that believe on his name (John 1:12). [Salvation comes through believing and receiving, not feeling.]

We are his witnesses of these things; and so is also the Holy Ghost, whom God hath given to them that obey him (Acts 5:32). [God promises His Holy Spirit to those who obey.]

But without faith it is impossible to please him; for he that cometh to God must believe that he is, and that he is a rewarder of them that diligently seek him (Heb. 11:6). [Faith in God will bring feelings we need.]

This is his commandment, That we should believe on the name of his Son Jesus Christ (1 John 3:23). [God commands us to have faith in Jesus.]

I said therefore unto you, that ye shall die in your sins: for if ye believe not that I am he, ye shall die in your sins (John 8:24).

They received not the love of the truth, that they might be saved. And for this cause God shall send them strong delusion, that they should believe a lie: That they all might be damned who believe not the truth (2 Thess. 2:10-12).

I will therefore put you in remembrance, though ye once knew this, how that the Lord, having saved the people out of the land of Egypt, afterward destroyed them that believed not (Jude 5).

He that believeth on the Son hath everlasting life: and he that believeth not the Son shall not see life; but the wrath of God abideth on him (John 3:36).

"I Am Afraid I Will Lose My Salvation"

For as many as are led by the Spirit of God, they are the sons of God. For ye have not received the spirit of bondage again to fear; but ye have received the Spirit of adoption, whereby we cry, Abba, Father. What shall we then say to these things? If God be for us, who can be against us? Who shall separate us from the love of Christ? shall tribulation, or distress, or persecution, or famine, or nakedness, or peril, or sword? As it is written, For thy sake we are killed all the day long; we are accounted as sheep for the slaughter. Nay, in all these things we are more than conquerors through him that loved us. For I am persuaded, that neither death, nor life, nor angels, nor principalities, nor powers, nor things present, nor things to come, nor height, nor depth, nor any other creature, shall be able to separate us from the love of God, which is in Christ Jesus our Lord (Rom. 8:14-15,31,35-39).

My sheep hear my voice, and I know them, and they follow me: And I give unto them eternal life; and they shall never perish, neither shall any man pluck them out of my hand. My Father, which gave them me, is greater than all; and no man is able to pluck them out of my Father's hand (John 10:27-29). [If a saved person could be lost, Jesus was mistaken.]

Now unto him that is able to keep you from

falling, and to present you faultless before the presence of his glory with exceeding joy (Jude 24). [If a saved person could be lost, the Bible is incorrect.]

Christ is become of no effect unto you, whosoever of you are justified by the law; ye are fallen from grace (Gal. 5:4). [If a church member is lost, he or she has depended upon works or keeping the Law rather than faith in Christ.]

I the Lord thy God will hold thy right hand, saying unto thee, Fear not; I will help thee (Isa. 41:13).

She shall bring forth a son, and thou shalt call his name Jesus: for he shall save his people from their sins (Matt. 1:21). [Jesus saves us; we don't save ourselves.]

There hath no temptation taken you but such as is common to man: but God is faithful, who will not suffer you to be tempted above that ye are able; but will with the temptation also make a way to escape, that ye may be able to bear it (1 Cor. 10:13). [There is nothing that comes your way that you cannot handle with God's help.]

Being confident of this very thing, that he which hath begun a good work in you will perform it until the day of Jesus Christ (Phil. 1:6). [God is the source of our strength.]

For the which cause I also suffer these things: nevertheless I am not ashamed: for I know whom I have believed, and am persuaded that he is able to keep that which I have committed unto him against that day (2 Tim. 1:12).

Whatsoever is born of God overcometh the world: and this is the victory that overcometh the world, even our faith (1 John 5:4).

Ye are of God, little children, and have overcome

them: because greater is he that is in you, than he that is in the world (1 John 4:4).

"I Plan to Accept Christ Someday, but Not Now"

Boast not thyself of to-morrow; for thou knowest not what a day may bring forth (Prov. 27:1).

He, that being often reproved hardeneth his neck, shall suddenly be destroyed, and that without remedy (Prov. 29:1).

The Lord said, My spirit shall not always strive with man, for that he also is flesh (Gen. 6:3).

My days are swifter than a weaver's shuttle, and are spent without hope (Job 7:6).

Behold, thou hast made my days as an handbreadth; and mine age is as nothing before thee: verily every man at his best state is altogether vanity (Ps. 39:5).

Go to now, ye that say, To-day or to-morrow we will go into such a city, and continue there a year, and buy and sell, and get gain: Whereas ye know not what shall be on the morrow. For what is your life? It is even a vapour, that appeareth for a little time, and then vanisheth away (Jas. 4:13-14).

The ground of a certain rich man brought forth plentifully: And he said, This will I do: I will pull down my barns, and built greater; and there will I bestow all my fruits and my goods. And I will say to my soul, Soul, thou hast much good things laid up for many years; take thine ease, eat, drink, and be merry. But God said unto him, Thou fool, this night thy soul shall be required of thee (Luke 12:16,18-20). [Life is uncertain. Death and judgment are certain.]

Man also knoweth not his time: as the fishes that are taken in an evil net, and as the birds that are caught in the snare; so are the sons of men snared in an evil time, when it falleth suddenly upon them (Eccl. 9:12).

A fool also is full of words: a man cannot tell what shall be; and what shall be after him, who can tell him? (Eccl. 10:14).

Watch therefore: for ye know not what hour your Lord doth come. But know this, that if the goodman of the house had known in what watch the thief would come, he would have watched, and would not have suffered his house to be broken up. Therefore be ye also ready: for in such an hour as ye think not the Son of man cometh (Matt. 24:42-44).

"Is the Bible Trustworthy?"

The grass withereth, the flower fadeth: but the word of our God shall stand for ever (Isa. 40:8).

For verily I say unto you, Till heaven and earth pass, one jot or one tittle shall in no wise pass from the law, till all be fulfilled (Matt. 5:18).

Heaven and earth shall pass away, but my words shall not pass away (Matt. 24:35).

The word of the Lord endureth for ever. And this is the word which by the gospel is preached unto you (1 Pet. 1:25).

For ever, O Lord, thy word is settled in heaven (Ps. 119:89).

The word of God is quick, and powerful, and sharper than any two-edged sword, piercing even to the dividing asunder of soul and spirit, and of the joints and marrow, and is a discerner of the thoughts and intents of the heart (Heb. 4:12).

Is not my word like as a fire? saith the Lord; and like a hammer that breaketh the rock in pieces? (Jer. 23:29).

Blessed be the Lord, that hath given rest unto his people Israel, according to all that he promised: there hath not failed one word of all his good promise, which he promised by the hand of Moses his servant (1 Kings 8:56).

All Scripture is given by inspiration of God, and is profitable for doctrine, for reproof, for correction, for instruction in righteousness (2 Tim. 3:16).

The prophecy came not in old time by the will of man: but holy men of God spake as they were moved by the Holy Ghost (2 Pet. 1:21).

Whatsoever things were written aforetime were written for our learning, that we through patience and comfort of the Scriptures might have hope (Rom. 15:4).

These things have I written unto you that believe on the name of the Son of God; that ye may know that ye have eternal life, and that ye may believe on the name of the Son of God (1 John 5:13).

"God Cannot Save Me; My Sins Are Too Great"

When Jesus heard that, he said unto them, They that be whole need not a physician, but they that are sick (Matt. 9:12).

The Lord is not slack concerning his promise, as some men count slackness; but is longsuffering to us-ward, not willing that any should perish, but that all should come to repentance (2 Pet. 3:9).

All that the Father giveth me shall come to me; and him that cometh to me I will in no wise cast out (John 6:37).

God commendeth his love toward us, in that, while we were yet sinners, Christ died for us (Rom. 5:8).

It shall come to pass, that whosoever shall call on the name of the Lord shall be saved (Acts 2:21).

Therefore as by the offence of one judgment came upon all men to condemnation; even so by the righteousness of one the free gift came upon all men unto justification of life (Rom. 5:18).

The publican, standing afar off, would not lift up so much as his eyes unto heaven, but smote upon his breast, saying, God be merciful to me a sinner. I tell you, this man went down to his house justified rather than the other: for every one that exalteth himself shall be abased; and he that humbleth himself shall be exalted (Luke 18:13-14).

Blessed be the God and Father of our Lord Jesus Christ, in whom we have redemption through his blood, the forgiveness of sins, according to the riches of his grace (Eph. 1:3,7).

To declare, I say, at this time his righteousness: that he might be just, and the justifier of him which believeth in Jesus (Rom. 3:26).

The Lord is not slack concerning his promise, as some men count slackness; but is longsuffering to us-ward, not willing that any should perish, but that all should come to repentance (2 Pet. 3:9).

The Spirit and the bride say, Come. And let him that heareth say, Come. And let him that is athirst come. And whosoever will, let him take the water of life freely (Rev. 22:17).

"I Have Tried and Failed"

Jesus answered him saying, It is written, That man shall not live by bread alone, but by every word of God (Luke 4:4). [Our strength comes from God.]

My sheep hear my voice, and I know them, and they follow me: And I give unto them eternal life; and they shall never perish, neither shall any man pluck them out of my hand. My Father, which gave them me, is greater than all; and no man is able to pluck them out of my Father's hand (John 10:27-28). [The believer is in the hand of Jesus, and Jesus is in God's hand.]

To them who by patient continuance in well-doing seek for glory and honour and immortality, eternal life (Rom. 2:7). [Eternal life comes to the one who patiently follows God's will.]

Let us not be weary in well-doing: for in due season we shall reap, if we faint not (Gal. 6:9). [There is spiritual reward in perseverance.]

I beseech you therefore, brethren, by the mercies of God, that ye present your bodies a living sacrifice, holy, acceptable unto God, which is your reasonable service. And be not conformed to this world: but be ye transformed by the renewing of your mind, that ye may prove what is that good, and acceptable, and perfect, will of God (Rom. 12:1-2). [Faithfulness in holy living will help one understand the will of God.]

Be careful for nothing; but in every thing by prayer and supplication with thanksgiving let your requests be made known unto God. And the peace of God, which passeth all understanding, shall keep your hearts and minds through Christ Jesus (Phil.

4:6-7). [Faithfulness in prayer will keep one from failure.]

If we confess our sins, he is faithful and just to forgive us our sins, and to cleanse us from all unrighteousness (1 John 1:9). [Confessing sins assures forgiveness.]

He that covereth his sins shall not prosper: but whoso confesseth and forsaketh them shall have mercy (Prov. 28:13). [Confessing sins brings God's mercy.]

As many as received him, to them gave he the power to become the sons of God, even to them that believe on his name (John 1:12).

Whosoever shall confess that Jesus is the Son of God, God dwelleth in him, and he in God (1 John 4:15).

"I Have Waited Too Long to Be Saved"

He [thief on cross] saith unto Jesus, Lord, remember me when thou comest into thy kingdom. And Jesus said unto him, Verily I say unto thee, To-day shalt thou be with me in paradise (Luke 23:42-43).[Christ gave salvation to a dying thief on the cross.]

God sent not his Son into the world to condemn the world; but that the world through him might be saved (John 3:17). [Christ's mission was to save all sinners.]

The thief cometh not, but for to steal, and to kill, and to destroy: I am come that they might have life, and that they might have it more abundantly (John 10:10). [Jesus came to give abundant life to all people.]

Whosoever drinketh of the water that I shall give

him shall never thirst; but the water that I shall give him shall be in him a well of water springing up into everlasting life (John 4:14). [Jesus came to quench the spiritual thirst of every person.]

I am the living bread which came down from heaven: if any man eat of this bread, he shall live for ever: and the bread that I will give is my flesh which I will give for the life of the world (John 6:51). [Jesus came to give living bread to any person.]

I am the door: by me if any man enter in, he shall be saved, and shall go in and out, and find pasture (John 10:9). [Jesus is the door of salvation for any person.]

Neither is there salvation in any other: for there is none other name under heaven given among men, whereby we must be saved (Acts 4:12). [Jesus is the Savior for all men everywhere in any circumstances.]

Soul-winners Are Made—Not Born

Soul-winning Is Christ's Plan for His Followers

Ye shall receive power, after that the Holy Ghost is come upon you: and ye shall be witnesses unto me both in Jerusalem, and in all Judea, and in Samaria, and unto the uttermost part of the earth (Acts 1:8).

I say unto thee, That thou art Peter, and upon this rock I will build my church; and the gates of hell shall not prevail against it (Matt. 16:18).

Howbeit Jesus suffered him not, but saith unto him, Go home to thy friends, and tell them how great things the Lord hath done for thee, and hath had compassion on thee (Mark 5:19).

I pray not that thou shouldest take them out of the world, but that thou shouldest keep them from the evil. As thou hast sent me into the world, even so have I also sent them into the world (John 17:15, 18).

For we are his workmanship, created in Christ Jesus unto good works, which God hath before ordained that we should walk in them (Eph. 2:10).

God, . . . hath reconciled us to himself by Jesus Christ, and hath given to us the ministry of reconciliation; Now then we are ambassadors for Christ, as though God did beseech you by us: we pray you in Christ's stead, be ye reconciled of God (2 Cor. 5:18,20).

He that taketh not his cross, and followeth after me is not worthy of me. He that findeth his life shall lose it: and he that loseth his life for my sake shall find it. He that receiveth you receiveth me, and he that receiveth me receiveth him that sent me (Matt. 10:38-40).

Soul-winning Is the Method God Chooses to Save People

For whosoever shall call upon the name of the Lord shall be saved. How then shall they call on him in whom they have not believed? and how shall they believe in him of whom they have not heard? (Rom. 10:13-14).

Then saith he unto his disciples, The harvest truly is plenteous, but the labourers are few; Pray ye therefore the Lord of the harvest, that he will send forth labourers into his harvest. (Matt. 9:37-38).

He that taketh not his cross, and followeth after me is not worthy of me. He that findeth his life shall lose it: and he that loseth his life for my sake shall find it. He that receiveth you receiveth me, and he that receiveth me receiveth him that sent me (Matt. 10:38-40).

When I say unto the wicked, O wicked man, thou shalt surely die; if thou dost not speak to warn the wicked from his way, that wicked man shall die in his iniquity; but his blood will I require at thine hand. Nevertheless, if thou warn the wicked of his way to turn from it; if he do not turn from his way, he shall die in his iniquity; but thou hast delivered thy soul (Ezek. 33:8-9).

Soul-winning Is the Example of Jesus

Jesus with an unexpected visitor (John 3, Nicodemus's conversion).

Jesus at a chance meeting (Luke 19:1-10, Zacchaeus in the tree).

Jesus resting at the well (John 4:28-29, a woman of Samaria).

Jesus at the cemetery (John 11:45, Jews at the burial of Lazarus).

Jesus at the sickbed (hospital) (Mark 5:1-20, insane man). Also man at the pool of Bethesda.

Jesus at tax time (Matt. 9:9, Matthew at the tax table).

Jesus at the work place (Matt. 4:21, James and John fishing).

Jesus at death (Luke 23:39-43, the thief on the cross).

Soul-winning Is the Example of New Testament Followers

John the Baptist (John 1:36-37).

Phillip with Nathanael (John 1:46-49).

Andrew with Peter: Andrew, . . . findeth his own brother Simon, and saith unto him, We have found the Messias (John 1:40-41).

Philip with the Ethiopia (Acts 8:26-39).

Persecuted Christians (Acts 8:4).

Peter and John at the Temple (Acts 3:19-20).

Paul and Onesimus (Philem. 1:10).

You Can Be a Soul-winner

All Christians Are to Be Soul-winners

Watch thou in all things, endure afflictions, do the work of an evangelist, make full proof of thy ministry (2 Tim. 4:5).

It pleased God by the foolishness of preaching to save them that believe (1 Cor. 1:21).

Whosoever shall call upon the name of the Lord shall be saved. How then shall they call on him in whom they have not believed? and how shall they believe in him of whom they have not heard? and how shall they hear without a preacher? And how shall they preach, except they be sent? as it is written, How beautiful are the feet of them that preach the gospel of peace, and bring glad tidings of good things! (Rom. 10:13-15).

God, that cannot lie, . . . hath is due times manifested his word through preaching (Titus 1:2-3).

How beautiful upon the mountains are the feet of him that bringeth good tidings, that publisheth peace; that bringeth good tidings of good, that publisheth salvation; that saith unto Zion, Thy God reigneth! Thy watchmen shall lift up the voice; with the voice together shall they sing: for they shall see eye to eye, when the Lord shall bring again Zion (Isa. 52:7-8).

How to Approach Persons You Want to Win

Use the telephone. Whenever possible, call for an appointment to visit in the home. Such a call prepares the people you will visit, and they are more likely to give a few minutes of uninterupted time.

Introduce yourself to the people with a smile. A smile opens doors and builds bonds between strangers. Look them in the eye. Call them by name. Your countenance should reveal genuine warmth.

Keep your conversations courteous and friendly; courtesy has a magnetic influence. Treat others as you want them to treat you. Let the law of kindness be on your tongue (Jas. 3:2).

Open the conversation with discussion focused on them. Show heartfelt interest in their background, their home, their family, and their occupation. They will appreciate your thoughtfulness.

Shift the conversation to spiritual matters. Talk briefly about God's goodness and love, the church, and your reason for visiting. Don't be afraid. They will respect your testimony.

Ask where they are attending church. Invite them to your church. Be sensitive to their conversation. Let them talk. You can quickly determine the extent of their understanding of salvation. If they give evidence that they have never been saved, ask if they will allow you to tell them what God has done to save them. Most will give you permission to explain God's plan of salvation.

How to Lead Persons to Christ

Lead them to see they are lost sinners. Gently but firmly make them aware of their sins and need for a Savior.

All have sinned, and come short of the glory of God (Rom. 3:23).

All we like sheep have gone astray; we have turned every one to his own way; and the Lord hath laid on him the iniquity of us all (Isa. 53:6).

We are all as an unclean thing, and all our righteousnesses are as filthy rags; and we all do fade as a leaf; and our iniquities, like the wind, have taken us away (Isa. 64:6).

He that believeth on him is not condemned: but he that believeth not is condemned already, because he hath not believed in the name of the only begotten Son of God (John 3:18).

Verily, verily, I say unto you, He that believeth on me hath everlasting life (John 6:47).

Lead them to repent of their sin. Repentance is turning away from sinful desires and expressing godly sorrow for sin.

The Lord is nigh unto them that are of a broken heart; and saveth such as be of a contrite spirit (Ps. 34:18).

Let the wicked forsake his way, and the unrighteous man his thoughts: and let him return unto the Lord, and he will have mercy upon him; and to our God, for he will abundantly pardon (Isa. 55:7).

If the wicked will turn from all his sins that he hath committed, and keep all my statutes, and do that which is lawful and right, he shall surely live, he shall not die (Ezek. 18:21).

I tell you, Nay: but, except ye repent, ye shall all likewise perish (Luke 13:3).

Repent ye therefore, and be converted, that your sins may be blotted out, when the times of refreshing shall come from the presence of the Lord (Acts 3:19).

Godly sorrow worketh repentance to salvation not to be repented of: but the sorrow of the world worketh death (2 Cor. 7:10).

The Lord is not slack concerning his promise, as some men count slackness; but is longsuffering to us-ward, not willing that any should perish, but that all should come to repentance (2 Pet. 3:9).

Lead them to trust Christ for forgiveness. Christ takes away the burden of sin and guilt. Trust involves belief in Him, commitment to Him.

Whosoever shall confess me before men, him shall the Son of man also confess before the angels of God (Luke 12:8).

The next day John seeth Jesus coming unto him, and saith, Behold the Lamb of God, which taketh away the sin of the world (John 1:29).

God so loved the world, that he gave his only begotten Son, that whosoever believeth in him should not perish, but have everlasting life (John 3:16).

The wages of sin is death; but the gift of God is eternal life through Jesus Christ our Lord (Rom. 6:23).

Now if any man have not the Spirit of Christ, he is none of his. And if Christ be in you, the body is dead because of sin; but the Spirit is life because of because of righteousness (Rom. 8:9-10).

God commendeth his love toward us, in that, while we were yet sinners, Christ died for us (Rom. 5:8).

If thou shalt confess with thy mouth the Lord Jesus, and shalt believe in thine heart that God hath raised him from the dead, thou shalt be saved (Rom. 10:9).

Whosoever shall call upon the name of the Lord shall be saved (Rom. 10:13).

Sirs, what must I do to be saved? And they said, Believe on the Lord Jesus Christ, and thou shalt be saved (Acts 16:30-31).

Lead them to confess their sins, their willingness to repent, and their trust in Christ. Ask them to pray and confess aloud to God and others present. The prayer need not be long, but it must be sincere. Frame a prayer for them if they are unfamiliar with prayer. Have them repeat each phrase after you: Dear Father,
I am a sinner. I am sorry for my sins. I ask Your forgiveness. Come into my heart now. Cleanse me. Save me. I do trust Your Son Jesus. I believe He died to pay the penalty for my sins. I believe He rose from the dead. I believe He lives today. I commit my life now and forever to Him. Amen.

I acknowledged my sin unto thee, and mine iniquity have I not hid. I said, I will confess my transgressions unto the Lord; and thou forgavest the iniquity of my sin (Ps. 32:5).

He that covereth his sins shall not prosper: but whoso confesseth and forsaketh them shall have mercy (Prov. 28:13).

Whosoever therefore shall confess me before

men, him will I confess also before my Father which is in heaven (Matt. 10:32).

With the heart man believeth unto righteousness; and with the mouth confession is made unto salvation. For the scripture saith, Whosoever believeth on him shall not be ashamed (Rom. 10:10-11).

If we confess our sins, he is faithful and just to forgive us our sins, and to cleanse us from all unrighteousness (1 John 1:9).

Whosoever shall confess that Jesus is the Son of God, God dwelleth in him, and he in God (1 John 4:15).

Lead them to unite with the church. Church membership is essential for Christian growth.

Those that be planted in the house of the Lord shall flourish in the courts of our God (Ps. 92:13).

I was glad when they said unto me, Let us go into the house of the Lord (Ps. 122:1).

Upon this rock I will build my church; and the gates of hell shall not prevail against it. And I will give unto thee the keys of the kingdom of heaven: and whatsoever thou shalt bind on earth shall be bound in heaven: and whatsoever thou shalt loose on earth shall be loosed in heaven (Matt. 16:18-19).

Then they that gladly received his word were baptized: and the same day there were added unto them [the church] about three thousand souls. And they continued stedfastly in the apostles' doctrine and fellowship, and in breaking of bread, and in prayers. And fear came upon every soul: and many wonders and signs were done by the apostles. And all that believed were together. And they, . . . did eat their meat with gladness and singleness of heart, Praising God, . . . And the Lord added to the church daily such as should be saved (Acts 2:41-44,46-47).

Let us hold fast the profession of our faith without wavering; . . . And let us consider one another to provoke unto love and to good works: Not forsaking the assembling of ourselves together, as the manner of some is; but exhorting one another: and so much the more, as ye see the day approaching (Heb. 10:23-25).

Conclude your visit after an appropriate length. Visits should be brief and considerate. Thirty minutes is usually long enough. Of course, stay longer if needed. If the persons make a profession of faith, congratulate them on their decision; ask them to share the decision with the church next Sunday. If they have not yet decided for Christ, leave the door open for further visits and discussion. Be gracious in your conversation with them. Never act condemnatory.

Leave with a brief prayer of thanksgiving and blessing. Most people will genuinely appreciate your thoughtful prayer.

How to Lead Children to Christ

Start Christian nurture very early in the life of the child.

Train up a child in the way he should go: and when he is old, he will not depart from it (Prov. 22:6).

Remember now thy Creator in the days of thy youth, while the evil days come not, nor the years draw nigh, when thou shalt say, I have no pleasure in them (Eccl. 12:1).

Ye fathers, provoke not your children to wrath:

but bring them up in the nurture and admonition of the Lord (Eph. 6:4).

Trust God to reveal to them their need of salvation.

The child Samuel ministered unto the Lord before Eli. The Lord called Samuel: and he answered, Here am I (1 Sam. 3:1,4).

Josiah was eight years old when he began to reign, . . . And he did that which was right in the sight of the Lord, . . . For in the eighth year of his reign, while he was yet young, he began to seek after the God of David his father (2 Chron. 34:1-3).

Behold, I was shaped in iniquity; and in sin did my mother conceive me (Ps. 51:5). [David acknowledged his sinful nature.]

Even a child is known by his doings, whether his work be pure, and whether it be right (Prov. 20:11). [God works with children.]

From a child thou hast known the holy scriptures, which are able to make these wise unto salvation through faith which is in Christ Jesus (2 Tim. 3:15). [Paul's reference to Timothy.]

Follow the leadership of the Holy Spirit. When children are ready to be saved, He will guide you and them.

Whosoever therefore shall humble himself as this little child, the same is greatest in the kingdom of heaven. And whoso shall receive one such little child in my name receiveth me. But whoso shall offend one of these little ones which believe in me, it were better for him that a millstone were hanged about his neck, and that he were drowned in the depth of the sea (Matt. 18:4-6). [Children have the capacity to be humble. Jesus commands us to be sensitive to their spiritual needs. They can believe in Him.]

Suffer the little children to come unto me, and forbid them not: for of such is the kingdom of God (Mark 10:14).

Share God's plan of salvation simply and revently. John 3:16 is appropriate to use with children.
God loves: "For God so loved"
God gave: "He gave his only begotten Son"
God invites: "Whosoever believeth in him"
God promises: Shall "not perish, but have everlasting life"

Have the child read the verse aloud. Break it down into the verse outline. Ask them to put their name in place of the word *whosoever.*

Another approach to use with children is the *ABC* method. There are three key words (italics by author):

A.   "*All* have sinned" (Rom. 3:23).
B.   "*Believe* on the Lord Jesus Christ" (Acts 16: 31).
C.   "*Confess* with thy mouth" (Rom. 10:9).

Invite children to become followers of Jesus. Never coerce. Trust God to draw them to salvation. Let them make the choice.

How to Approach Those Who Resent Being Approached

Live your life as an example of Christ likeness. All about you are people who know full well they are lost, but they resent any questions about their relationship to Christ. They will respect your Christian example; you are the best Christian someone knows. Your life speaks powerfully and eloquently when it is lived as a testimony to Christ's work (Rom. 12:1-2).

Launch a campaign of prayer. God really does answer prayer. "I say unto you, Ask, and it shall be given you; seek, and ye shall find; knock, and it shall be opened unto you" (Luke 11:9). Enlist other Christians to pray with your for a specific person. A prayer partnership will encourage you to keep on praying. Have faith that God knows your petition. "It shall come to pass, that before they call, I will answer; and while they are yet speaking, I will hear" (Isa. 65:24).

Search for the appropriate person to win the resentful. A friend may have the key to unlock the heart of the unsaved. Perhaps a relative or loved one can best share. Be patient. God has someone to give His message. Your task is to be spiritually alert and sensitive to determine the one God will send. Of course, it could be you whom God chooses to approach the angry one. If so, claim this promise. "They that sow in tears shall reap in joy. He that goeth forth and weepeth, bearing precious seed, shall doubtless come again with rejoicing, bringing his sheaves with him" (Ps. 126:5-6).

Seek a time when you can share one-to-one without interruption. Angry people are less likely to show resentment in a one-to-one situation. They may tend to feel attacked if two people visit at once, and they are not likely to reveal the real reason for their resentment. The solo approach is a demonstration of warm personal care and concern. Uninterrupted time affords them the opportunity to talk, to vent pent-up frustrations and resentment, and to focus on what really is bothering them. Be nondefensive in your approach no matter what they may say to you. "A soft answer turneth away wrath: but grevious words stir up anger" (Prov. 15:1).

Claim the promise that God is with you. He is with us even "unto the end of the world" (Matt. 28:20). "Therefore, my beloved brethren, be ye steadfast, unmoveable, always abounding in the work of the Lord, forasmuch as ye know that your labour is not in vain in the Lord" (1 Cor. 15:58).

How to Use the Bible in Soul-winning

Carry a Bible or New Testament on every soul-winning visit. If you feel awkward visiting with complete Bible in hand, carry a New Testament. Some New Testaments are small enough to fit easily into a pocket or a purse. As the visit progresses, share from the Bible. The presence of God's Word will help keep the conversation from straying from your mission.

Sit close to the prospects, so you can point out Scripture references. When you quote Scripture, it is wise to indicate where the passage is found. Look up the references and point to where the verse is located. Let them see that you are accurate in your quotation.

Ask the seekers to read aloud two or three key salvation passages. There is power in opening and reading the Bible. If the persons have difficulty in reading, quickly take over the reading for them. If the unsaved friends have a Bible in the room, it is effective to have them read from their own Bibles. This puts them at ease since it indicates they already have respect for God's Word.

Explain the meaning of the verses read. Be familiar with vital salvation passages. Familiarity with a few well chosen verses will help your hearers. Too many references may confuse.

To demonstrate the sinfulness of people, use Romans 3:23: "For all have sinned, and come short of the glory of God." Ask what *all* means.

To demonstrate the need for repentance, read Acts 16:25-31. Tell the story of the sinful jailer. Relate his question in verse 30, and let the unsaved person read the answer in verse 31.

To demonstrate the need for confessing Christ as Savior and Lord, read Matthew 10:32-33. Emphasize the words *confess* and *deny.*

Treat the Bible reverently at all times. It is God's treasure.

Provide a copy of the Bible to all those who do not have one.

Bible Promises and Church Membership

Christians Are to Be United with the Church

They that gladly received his word were baptized: and the same day there were added unto them about three thousand souls. And they continued stedfastly in the apostles' doctrine and fellowship, and in breaking of bread, and in prayers (Acts 2:41-42). [Believers were baptized and grew in doctrine, fellowship, and prayer.]

The husband is the head of the wife, even as Christ is the head of the church: and he is the saviour of the body (Eph. 5:23).

He is the head of the body, the church: who is the beginning, the firstborn from the dead; that in all things he might have the preeminence (Col. 1:18).

Husbands, love your wives, even as Christ also

loved the church, and gave himself for it (Eph. 5:25).

So we, being many, are one body in Christ, and every one members one of another (Rom. 12:5). [The church is the body of Christ, and we have unity in him.]

Now ye are the body of Christ, and members in particular (1 Cor. 12:27). [Christians are part of the body of Christ, but each has his or her own particular work.]

He gave some, apostles; and some, prophets; and some, evangelists; and some, pastors and teachers; For the perfecting of the saints, for the work of the ministry, for the edifying of the body of Christ (Eph. 4:11-12). [Christians (saints) are to take part in the work of the ministry.]

If ye continue in the faith grounded and settled, and be not moved away from the hope of the gospel, which ye have heard, and which was preached to every creature which is under heaven; whereof I Paul am made a minister; Who now rejoice in my sufferings for you, and fill up that which is behind of the afflictions of Christ in my flesh for his body's sake, which is the church (Col. 1:23-24). [Paul suffered for the church. So should we be willing.]

I say also unto Thee, That thou art Peter, and upon this rock I will build my church; and the gates of hell shall not prevail against it (Matt. 16:18). [Jesus established the church.]

Now therefore ye are no more strangers and foreigners, but fellow-citizens with the saints, and of the household of God; and are built upon the foundation of the apostles and prophets, Jesus Christ himself being the chief corner stone; in whom all the building fitly framed together groweth unto an holy temple in the Lord (Eph. 2:19-21). [Christians are parts of the building.]

Ye also, as lively stones, are built up a spiritual house, an holy priesthood, to offer up spiritual sacrifices, acceptable to God by Jesus Christ (1 Pet. 2:5). [Christians are living stones in God's church.]

Bible Promises and Christian Service

Christians Are to Be Committed Servants of Christ

Therefore, my beloved brethren, be ye stedfast, unmoveable, always abounding in the work of the Lord, forasmuch as ye know that your labour is not in vain in the Lord (1 Cor. 15:58).

Whosoever will be great among you, shall be your minister: And whosoever of you will be the chiefest, shall be servant of all (Mark 10:43-44).

Let us not be weary in well-doing: for in due season we shall reap, if we faint not (Gal. 6:9).

Work out your own salvation with fear and trembling. For it is God which worketh in you both to will and to do of his good pleasure (Phil. 2:12-13).

Whosoever shall give you a cup of water to drink in my name, because ye belong to Christ, Verily I say unto you, he shall not lose his reward (Mark 9:41).

Brethren, ye have been called unto liberty; only use not liberty for an occasion to the flesh, but by love serve one another (Gal. 5:13).

Bear ye one another's burdens, and so fulfill the law of Christ (Gal. 6:2).

As we have therefore opportunity, let us do good unto all men, especially unto them who are of the household of faith (Gal. 6:10).

If I then, your Lord and Master, have washed your feet; ye also ought to wash one another's feet (John 13:14).

Wherefore we receiving a kingdom which cannot be moved, let us have grace, whereby we may serve God acceptably with reverence and godly fear (Heb. 12:28).